Graciela

GRACIELA

A Mexican-American

Child Tells Her Story

by Joe Molnar

Franklin Watts, Inc. · *845 Third Avenue · New York, New York 10022*
1972

SBN-531-02023-1

Copyright © 1972 by Joe Molnar

Library of Congress Catalog Card Number: 77-182297

Printed in the United States of America

The text of this book is based on tape recordings of conversations with Graciela.

My name is Graciela and I'm twelve years old. I live in a small town in Texas. I live there with my mother and father and my seven brothers and two sisters. The names of my brothers and sisters are Eleazar, Jose Junior, Juan, David, Moises, Abel, the baby Noe, Maria, and Irma.

My brothers and sisters, all of us that are big enough, we help mother and father around the house as much as we can. Sometimes I go out and water the plants or help my father wash the truck, or I pick up the leaves in the yard or help clean the house inside.

I like best to take care of Noe the baby. I play with him, make his bottle, and change his dirty diaper and feed him.

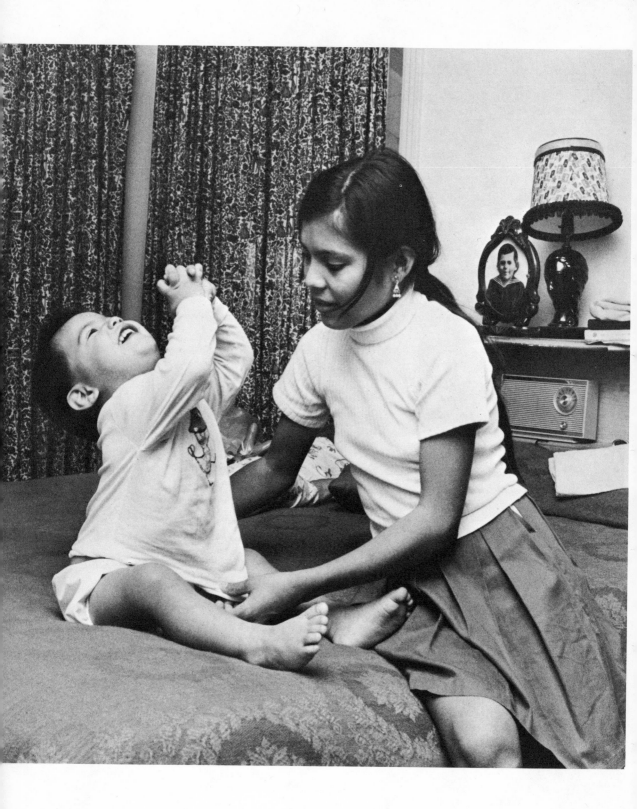

If mother is very busy in the kitchen, I help to wash the dishes or help her to prepare the food. She makes a lot of Mexican meals of course. Tacos are my favorite. You start out with a tortilla, that's like a pancake, and on the tortilla you put ground beef or chicken and tomatoes and onions and lettuce and wrap it all up and it tastes oh so good! We eat a lot of rice and beans too. And caldo, that's a soup with rice and chicken in it.

My favorite sister is Maria and she's sixteen years old. She works in a restaurant in our town, but only on Saturdays and Sundays. She's a waitress. She gets up about five in the morning to go to work, and makes about three dollars a day and maybe another three dollars in tips. Of course she gives most of the money to my mother and father. With the rest she saves up and buys clothes for herself.

In the restaurant Maria serves and takes orders and takes cash and washes the dishes and does just about everything. She comes home awful tired sometimes, but she sits down and does the schoolwork she has to do. Maria is smart and I think she's going to finish school and try to go to college.

My brother Abel he's three years old and last week I was very upset because something awful happened to him. I was inside the house and my mother came running from outside and told me to get her a towel quick and she said that Abel was hurt and bleeding. I ran fast and got the towel and saw my brother sitting on the ground touching his head and his leg was hurt bad. My mother said a motorcycle ran into him. And we all got very scared and called the ambulance. And the ambulance took him to the hospital.

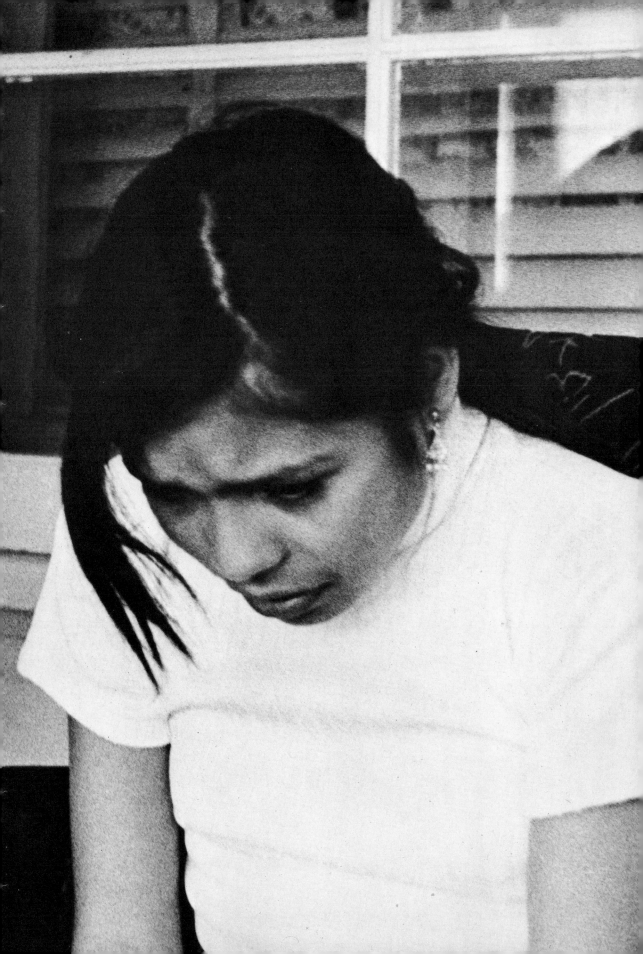

The next day, when I saw him in the hospital, he was smiling a little and feeling better. I felt good to see him smiling and stayed with him right there to give him some food. Then we watched TV a little and he started to get sleepy. I asked my mother and father if I could spend the night there and they said yes. I got a pillow and a blanket, covered myself in a chair, and went to sleep. It was kind of scary, sleeping all night in the hospital, nobody in the room but my brother and me.

Two days later Maria called my mother and said the hospital told her we could take my brother home but we had to pay first. And the hospital said we owed them two hundred dollars and Abel would have to stay there until we paid. I got very upset when I heard that and thought the hospital was ignorant and mean. But later, on the telephone, the hospital said yes, we could take him home and we brought Abel home the next day. Now he's much better, but sometimes his leg still hurts and the bandage we haven't taken it off yet.

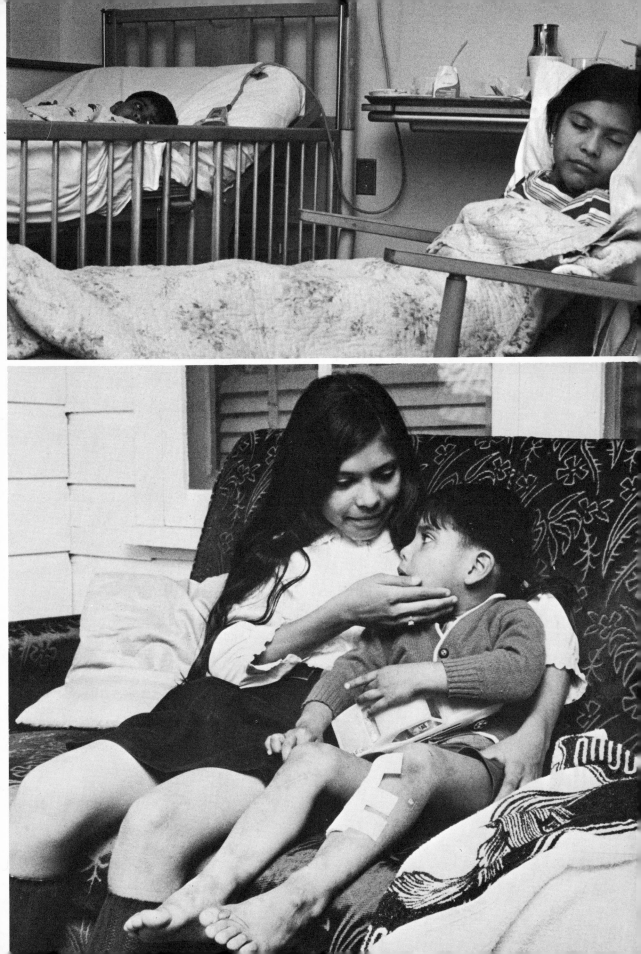

At the beginning of June we go north to Michigan to work in the fields picking fruits and vegetables. School isn't over yet, but we have to go because we need the money. My little brothers will be able to finish their classes in Michigan for the month of June, but the rest of us won't. My grandmother comes with us in the truck, she is the one who takes care of the little kids. When we get there we stay in the house the farmer gives us. It's very small, only two rooms for our whole family. And it's missing a lot. If you want hot water you have to heat it up and the stove it only has two burners and no oven. And you have to go outside to a well to get the water with a pump.

My mother and me, we go out to one field. My father, Eleazar, Irma, and Maria go to another field. They pick tomatoes, watermelons, beans, cucumbers, squash, and pickles. Pickles are the worst, because you have to be bending down all the time and get all wet, pickle plants have a lot of water. My mother and me, we pick cauliflower. We get a big bunch and separate them and put them in baskets.

We all start at seven in the morning and work until noon. Then we go back to the house for lunch or sometimes eat in the field. About one o'clock we start working again until four or five. We're very tired when we finish and come home, our waists hurt and our hands. We get paid a dollar fifty an hour. After working in the fields three months I think we bring home about three thousand dollars. Father says that's not a lot of money because, until the next summer, we have to live and pay most of our bills from that money. There's only a little work for us in our town in Texas.

The people in Michigan seem to like Mexican-Americans. They are real friendly to us. We go to a store and they look at us and everything like that but after a while they become more talkative and nice to us. Here in Texas it's different. They just won't come straight out and tell you they don't like you. They'll just kind of show it. They'll go their own way and tell you to go your way. Or like in school they won't talk to you sometimes, just sort of leave you out. Anyhow most of the bad feeling comes from a few teachers.

Like last year one of the teachers brought his little daughter to school, she was about three years old. And she was crying and one of the kids asked the teacher why she was crying and the teacher said it was because she had never seen Mexicans before. Well, maybe it was true but the teacher shouldn't have said it that way. Another time a teacher in the high school called my brother Eleazar a wetback, and he doesn't like to be called that. He says he's a Chicano, a Mexican-American who's proud of it. But most of the teachers are nice and treat the kids okay.

My father, when we are not in the north working in the fields, he goes to Texas State Technical In-
stitute to study. He is in a special program that helps
Mexican-Americans to learn skills that will get them
good jobs. He is trying to improve his English too
while he studies radio and television, he wants to be
a repairman or mechanic. So he studies hard and hopes
to get his diploma because like in certain jobs they
require it, your diploma, and if you don't have it,
well, even though you might know what you're
doing, they still won't take you without your diploma.

Sometimes my mother and father worry a lot. They worry about sending us to school. They want very much for us to finish school and not to have to take us out just so we can work. They try their best to give us clothes and dress us up real good so we can go to school neat and proud. They worry about feeding our family too. And getting another bed so my little brother David doesn't have to sleep on a mattress on the floor. So they worry about money a lot. Right now we have enough to pay our bills. We are paying off the house, and in two more years it will belong to us. And we are paying off our truck, we're almost through with that and it's a big bill too, about ninety-five dollars a month. Our biggest worry right now is how to pay the hospital for Abel. But we'll be okay. We'll manage.

I play a lot with my friends and my brothers and sisters. We play chase and hide-and-seek and a lot of games that we think up ourselves.

I like to dance too and I'll dance anyplace, if there's no music I don't care, indoors or outside, at home, at school, my friend's house, really anyplace. Once, in school, the teacher went out of the room for a while and gave us permission to play some records. And I started playing them and dancing very wild and some of my friends started dancing wild too and laughing and everything.

Today my mother and father and Maria and me, we went to the carnival in Brownsville, that's a big town right across the border from Mexico. We played a lot of games and won some prizes. One game, we had to get a ball inside a ring and I did it and won a stuffed little dog. Maria and mother won some plates and a cup by throwing nickels so they landed in the center of the plates. We went on a lot of great rides too. The ride we liked best, first we went real slow and then we went all of a sudden real fast and I got scared but my sister was laughing.

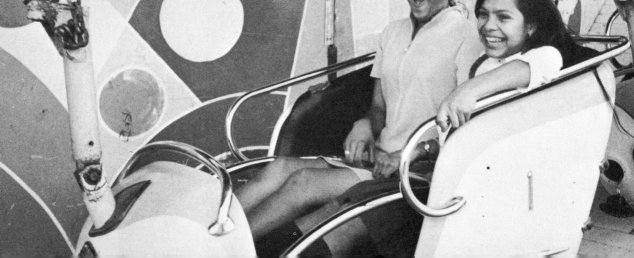

Then we went into a fun house and the steps on the floor would move and I almost fell and I was laughing so hard my stomach ached. But in the hall of mirrors I laughed the hardest. We couldn't find where the door was leading out and went round and round bumping into mirrors until we found the door. Then we bought some cotton candy and coke and apple candy, real delicious, and then we came home.

Sometimes I wish I was already in high school or I wish I was already a nurse and working. Then maybe I could have a piano. More than anything I want a piano. I would study and learn how to play it real good. I would play happy music. Music like it would make me feel everything is okay, everything is going to be all right.

Joe Molnar is a native New Yorker and in 1952 graduated from Queens College. He was an elementary-school teacher when he bought his first camera a few years ago, with no intention other than becoming a good amateur photographer. Within months, however, he became so involved with photography that it became a full-time interest, and he decided to devote himself to photojournalism. Mr. Molnar has two books forthcoming on Australian subjects, the result of an extended visit to that country.